TRAINEE
WORKBOOK

Reducing the Risk

3rd Edition

KEEPING YOUR MINISTRY
SAFE FROM CHILD
SEXUAL ABUSE

Richard R. Hammar, J.D., LL.M., CPA
and Marian V. Liautaud

YOUR
CHURCH

REDUCING THE RISK 3RD EDITION
Keeping Your Ministry Safe from Child Sexual Abuse
Trainee Workbook

©2008 by Christianity Today International

ISBN-10: 0-917463-42-0

ISBN-13: 978-0-917463-42-6

Published by Your Church Resources
Christianity Today International
465 Gundersen Drive
Carol Stream, IL 60188
(630) 260-6200
E-mail: RTRcustserv@christianitytoday.com

CREDITS

Edited by: Marian V. Liautaud

Cover design: Mary Bellus

Text design: Mary Bellus

We gratefully acknowledge the contribution James F. Cobble, Jr. and Steven Klipowicz made developing the original *Reducing the Risk*.

10 9 8 7 6 5 4 3 2 1   09 08 07

Printed in the United States of America

This book presents suggestions that may help you reduce the risk of child sexual abuse within your ministry or organization. Unfortunately, no foolproof procedure exists to eliminate child sexual abuse. It is possible that an incident may occur even if you implement all the suggestions in this book. You are encouraged to review this resource carefully and to consult a local attorney to receive advice concerning your prevention efforts.

This publication is designed to provide accurate and authoritative information in regard to the subject matter covered. It is sold with the understanding that the publisher is not engaged in rendering legal, accounting, or other professional service. If legal advice or other expert assistance is required, the services of a competent professional person should be sought. "From a Declaration of Principles jointly adopted by a Committee of the American Bar Association and a Committee of Publishers and Associations."

TABLE OF CONTENTS

FOREWORD

WESLEY HAD A HARD TIME telling me his story the first time we met. We sat sipping coffee, and he struggled to find the words to describe what had taken place between him and his former youth pastor nearly seven years earlier. Slowly, he shared the grooming and eventual sexual abuse his perpetrator—a man he fully trusted—committed against him. As an older teen when the abuse occurred, Wesley spent years blaming himself for the outcome of this relationship. Now as an adult, he still admits to being rebellious toward his parents. At the same time, he wonders, where was the church? What was their role in protecting him?

We set out to address these questions when we launched into remaking *Reducing the Risk* 3rd Edition. No child should ever experience the trauma of sexual abuse—and certainly never in a church or ministry setting. Sadly, there are hundreds of allegations made each year over incidents of child sexual abuse in faith communities. In fact, churches, by virtue of their open, welcoming nature, often attract predators looking for a low-resistance environment where they can prey on children.

Since the 1980s, when allegations of clergy sexual abuse became widely publicized, people have become far less tolerant of churches that fail to provide safeguards against child sexual abuse. *Reducing the Risk* was born in 1993, when Richard Hammar, James Cobble, and Steven Klipowicz created comprehensive resources to help make ministries safe from child sexual abuse. Because of their work, countless faith communities have learned about the need to properly screen and select workers, and to implement solid supervision policies for their children's and youth ministry.

2008 marks the 15-year anniversary of *Reducing the Risk*. When we began to revise and update the new 3rd edition, our mission was clear: Create a turn-key kit for churches to implement a child sexual abuse prevention program. The Training DVD, Leader's Guide, Trainee Workbook, and Screening Forms & Records File for Volunteers provide everything you need to help keep kids safe in your ministry.

We know you love kids. We do, too. We've poured our hearts into making this the best training on protecting kids from sexual abuse within a faith community. Our vision is that no child—and no ministry—would ever fall victim to the devastating effects of sexual abuse.

Marian V. Liautaud
Editor

HOW TO USE THIS TRAINEE WORKBOOK

THIS TRAINEE WORKBOOK is designed to be used in conjunction with the *Reducing the Risk* Training DVD. Together, these resources provide the information and guidance you'll need to enforce and comply with your ministry's child protection program.

This Trainee Workbook targets two specific audiences: Ministry Leaders and Children's/Youth Workers.

As a Ministry Leader, you'll receive comprehensive instruction on the issues surrounding child sexual abuse and how to prevent it. This training is designed to fully equip you to enforce a child protection program and to train staff and volunteers who work with minors, such as Sunday school teachers, children's ministry workers, and youth volunteers.

If you are a Children's/Youth Worker, this training provides everything you need to properly supervise and interact with kids. The Trainee Workbook is designed as a companion tool to help you follow along with, and gain a broader understanding of, the material presented in the DVD training segments.

Each chapter in this workbook corresponds to the Training DVD. We've provided plenty of room for you to take notes and jot down questions. We've also included fill-in-the-blank sentences to reinforce key points in the training. After you've completed the training, you can take the test in the back of this workbook. Your supervisor may retain your completed test in your service folder, and you may be asked to repeat child protection training on a periodic basis.

TRAINING DVD:

Ten video presentations are included on your Training DVD. This DVD is ideal for training individuals, small groups, or your entire congregation. The DVD engages both the head and heart, offering personal stories along with practical, how-to teaching. To get started, go to "Start Training Tracks" on the Training DVD. Select the appropriate track for your ministry role. Depending on your role, you may not have to view every segment. Here's what's covered in the videos:

Video #1. "Child Protection as the Foundation of Your Ministry." This segment gets people invested in the training that follows. It provides an overview of the problem of child sexual abuse in the church and ministries. It should be the first presentation that you view and show.

Video #2. "A Victim's Story." This segment presents the true story of a victim of clergy abuse. It should help sensitize leaders to the human cost of sexual abuse in ministry settings.

Video #3. "Sexual Abuse in Faith Communities—an Expert Roundtable." This presentation features five experts who deal with different aspects of sexual abuse in the faith community, ranging from a psychologist who helped create his church's child protection program to an insurance claims manager who understands the legal impact of sexual abuse allegations. By sitting in on this group's discussion, viewers gain insight into the issues surrounding child sexual abuse in ministries today.

Video #4. "Testimony of a Sex Offender." Viewers will hear from a convicted sex offender. As you'll learn through his story, there's no sure way to know who is or isn't a sex offender.

Video #5. "Screening & Selection: Your First Line of Defense (with Richard Hammar)." Richard Hammar, noted church attorney and CPA, and one of the creators of *Reducing the Risk*, presents a powerful teaching session on the importance of proper screening and selection of staff and volunteers. This segment lays out five key ways to reduce liability.

Video #6. "Screening & Selection: The Candidate (a short film)." This segment creatively teaches leaders how to interview a candidate, conduct a background check, and check references. Participants will see and hear what the screening and selection process should look like.

Video #7. "Legal Requirements: The Church's Responsibility to Protect Kids (with Richard Hammar)" Viewers receive more training by the most trusted name in church law—Richard Hammar. In this segment, he explains legal requirements for protecting children in your ministry, plus practical tips on how your ministry can meet the "reasonable standard of care."

Video #8. "Supervising Scenarios: What Would You Do?" This fast-paced, interactive segment teaches principles of good supervision. It helps children's and youth workers think through common scenarios of supervision.

Video #9. "Responding to an Allegation." What would your ministry do if it were faced with an allegation of child sexual abuse? This video depicts the story of how one church handled this situation. Experts add insights to this first-person story.

Video #10. "Taking the Next Steps." Spokesperson David Staal wraps up the DVD and offers action steps to implement or strengthen your child protection program.

ADDITIONAL REDUCING THE RISK RESOURCES

SCREENING FORMS & RECORDS FILE FOR VOLUNTEERS:

This important tool ensures that key aspects of the screening process are performed and well documented. Inside you'll find all of the resources you need for screening individual volunteers who will be working with the children and youth in your ministry. This resource includes a Volunteer Service Application, interview forms with recommended questions, reference check forms for volunteers, and an area to annually review and update Volunteer Service Application. The entire booklet is designed to be used as your filing system for all screening information about the individual trainee, helping you keep all critical documentation in a single location.

ONLINE SUPPORT AT REDUCINGTHERISK.COM:

This coordinating website offers additional support for implementing the *Reducing the Risk* materials. You'll find all of the video segments online, in addition to discussion boards and a complete resource library. Using the website allows you to train your volunteers or staff if you don't own the Training DVD, or to train any people that might have missed your scheduled training day. (**ReducingTheRisk.com** is an additional fee).

CHAPTER ONE

For Ministry Leaders:

MAKING SAFETY YOUR TOP PRIORITY

Creating a Safe Environment

Let the little children come to me, and do not hinder them, for the Kingdom of God belongs to such as these. (Luke 18:16)

Training Overview

For Ministry Leaders (approximately 4 hours)

WHAT'S THE GOAL OF THIS TRAINING?

- To increase awareness of the symptoms and consequences of child sexual abuse.
- To underscore the ministry's vulnerability to child sexual abuse.
- To create an understanding of liability concerns and ministry policy guidelines pertaining to screening, supervision, and reporting.
- To provide instruction on worker selection and worker training.

WHO SHOULD ATTEND?

All paid or volunteer ministry leaders who oversee children or youth activities, including the following:

- Nursery supervisor
- Day care director
- Leader of club programs
- Youth ministers and sponsors
- Sunday School superintendents and departmental leaders
- VBS director
- Children's choral director
- Christian school principals
- Other ministry leaders working with children or youth

WHAT WILL I NEED TO PARTICIPATE IN THIS TRAINING?

- *Reducing the Risk* Trainee Workbook and pen

- *Reducing the Risk* Training DVD or online access to **ReducingTheRisk.com** if you are training individually

- *Reducing the Risk* Leader's Guide if you are a ministry leader training yourself in child protection

Let's Get Started

Go to "Start Training Tracks" on the Training DVD. Select **"For Child Advocates & Ministry Leaders."**

- **View Video #1: "Child Protection as the Foundation of Your Ministry."**

Notes:

OPEN FOR DISCUSSION

- What led you to serve in your area of ministry?

- Effective ministry can only take place if a child feels safe. How safe do you think kids feel when they come to your Sunday school or other ministry programs? What does your ministry do to ensure children's safety?

- In the opening video, the children's leader checked in each child by giving them a special bracelet to identify them. What check-in procedure does your ministry use to ensure kids leave with the correct adult?

■ Did you resonate with any of the objections you heard in the opening video? Could you envision others in your ministry voicing these or other objections?

Fill in the blanks:

When it comes to _____, many people still don't believe that the _____ is real.

When a child has a good ministry experience, they're more likely to _____ in their faith and stay

involved with the _____. When a child is a victim of sexual abuse in a faith community,

the _____ are devastating and last the child's _____.

You will be viewing a story of a youth who was victimized by his youth pastor. As you'll see, one case of abuse can have an incredible impact on individuals, their families, and the faith community.

■ **View Video #2: "A Victim's Story."** *(This video may be difficult for some people to watch. Although this segment is not graphic in its description of sexual abuse, it may elicit strong emotions if you have experienced abuse or you know loved ones who have endured this trauma.)*

Notes:

OPEN FOR DISCUSSION:

- At the beginning of Wesley's story, what were some signs of a healthy relationship between a student and his youth pastor? What were clues that the relationship was not healthy?

- In your ministry, what do you do to monitor and hold staff and workers accountable for their behavior?

- Teens are highly susceptible to sexual abuse. Ministries tend to loosen their safety policies as kids get older, mistakenly believing kids will be able to discern dangerous individuals or situations. What's your reaction to Wesley's story? What responsibility do you think the church had to him and his family?

- How do you think Wesley's family felt when no one at their church believed their allegations? (You'll learn more about how to respond to an allegation later in this training.)

If teens are vulnerable to predators, how much more so young children! It's up to adults to provide protective boundaries to keep minors from being exposed to harmful individuals.

Fill in the blanks:

For Wesley, child sexual abuse _____ his relationship with _____. Wesley's story is

tragic, but it shares a common thread that links him to other victims: You cannot tell who is or who isn't

a _____. Although Wesley was an older teen when his abuse occurred, as

a _____, it was not his responsibility to _____ himself. Children, whether they are 7

or 17, are not expected to use perfect _____. This is one of the main reasons our legal system

entrusts children to _____ care.

Going Deeper ○ ○ ○ ○ ○ ○

Consequences of Child Sexual Abuse

Child sexual abuse robs children of their childhood and can potentially scar its young victims for life. Too often in the past, the effects of abuse were minimized or dismissed. Children were viewed as being resilient. But recent research has shown that children can suffer significant pain from even a single abusive incident. Faith communities must be aware of the pain and long-term suffering that can accompany such abuse. Abused children can display a wide range of negative symptoms in the aftermath of abuse, including abnormal fears, post-traumatic stress disorder (PTSD), aggressive behavior, sexual acting out, depression, diffused sexual identity, and poor self-esteem (Kendall-Tackett, Williams, and Finkelhor, 1991). The incidence of sexually transmitted disease is also a possible outcome.

The degree of damage depends upon several factors, including the intensity, duration, and frequency of the abuse. In addition, the relationship of the perpetrator to the child matters. If the abuser is a known and trusted authority figure in the child's life, the degree of impact increases dramatically.

Consequences of child sexual abuse can plague victims into adulthood. Outcome studies of adult survivors of child sexual abuse suggest the following effects: sexual dysfunction, eating disorders, substance abuse, promiscuity, disassociation from emotions, and possible perpetration of sexual abuse on others (Geffner, 1992).

As we saw in Video #2, **"A Victim's Story,"** when ministry leaders, pastors, and respected congregational workers perpetrate the abuse, lifelong religious confusion and deep feelings of enmity toward God and the church can also occur.

o   o   o

■ **View Video #3: "Sexual Abuse in Faith Communities—An Expert Roundtable"**

This DVD segment features five experts who deal with different aspects of sexual abuse in faith communities. You'll hear from a risk manager who helps develop safety resources for churches and faith-based programs, a staff psychologist who helped create his church's child protection program, an insurance claims manager who understands the legal impact of sexual abuse allegations, a clinical psychologist who specializes in counseling victims of sexual abuse, and an insurance industry leader who works among faith communities of every denomination.

Notes:

OPEN FOR DISCUSSION:

■ Do you think faith communities are more at risk for being sued today than they were 20 years ago? Why or why not?

■ What are the factors that make faith communities and ministries particularly vulnerable?

■ If you were to put on an "offender eye," what area of your ministry might be vulnerable?

- Which vulnerabilities are easiest to correct? Which would be most difficult to correct?

- If you can't identify a sex offender based on outward appearances and impressions, what can you do to protect children from being victims?

Going Deeper o o o o o o

What is Child Sexual Abuse?

Part of supporting the creation of a child protection program is understanding what child sexual abuse actually is. The precise legal definition of child sexual abuse or molestation varies from state to state, but it usually includes any form of sexual contact or exploitation in which a minor is being used for the sexual stimulation of the perpetrator. In a more general sense, child sexual abuse is:

Any sexual activity with a child whether in the home by a caretaker, in a day care situation, a foster/residential setting, or in any other setting, including on the street by a person unknown to the child. The abuser may be an adult, an adolescent, or another child, provided the child is four years older than the victim (National Resource Center on Child Sexual Abuse).

Child sexual abuse may be violent or non-violent, but all child sexual abuse is an exploitation of a child's vulnerability and powerlessness in which the abuser is fully responsible for the actions. Child sexual abuse is criminal behavior that involves children in sexual behaviors for which they are not personally, socially, and developmentally ready.

Child sexual abuse includes behaviors that involve aspects of both touching and non-touching.

Types of abuse that involve touching include:

- fondling
- oral, genital, and anal penetration
- intercourse
- forcible rape

Types of sexual abuse that do not involve touching include:

- verbal comments
- pornographic videos
- obscene phone calls
- exhibitionism
- allowing children to witness sexual activity

The full extent of child sexual abuse in our country is not known. Conservative estimates suggest that between 500,000 and 1,500,000 children are sexually abused each year, although the actual number is likely to be higher because the greater percentage of these cases go unreported. A national retrospective study on the prevalence of child sexual abuse found that 27 percent of adult women and 16 percent of men claimed to have experienced some form of child sexual victimization. Over 25 percent indicated this occurred before the age of nine (Finkelhor, Hotaling, Lewis, and Smith, 1990).

Child sexual abuse occurs in all demographic, racial, ethnic, socio-economic, and religious groups. Strangers account for less than 20 percent of the abusers. Estimates indicate that when a known assailant commits the abuse, half of the time it is a father or stepfather, and the rest of the time it is a trusted adult who misuses his or her authority over children.

o   o   o

Going Deeper · · · · · ·

Symptoms of Molestation

Ministry workers and staff members should be alert to the physical signs of abuse and molestation, as well as to the behavioral and verbal signs a victim may exhibit. Some of the more common signs are summarized below (Sloan, 1983).

Physical signs may include:

- lacerations and bruises
- nightmares
- irritation, pain, or injury to the genital area
- difficulty with urination
- discomfort when sitting
- torn or bloody underclothing
- venereal disease

Behavioral signs may include:

- anxiety when approaching the ministry
- nervous or hostile behavior toward adults
- sexual self-consciousness
- "acting out" of sexual behavior
- withdrawal from ministry activities and friends

Verbal signs may include the following statements:

- "I don't like [a particular ministry worker]."
- "[A ministry worker] does things to me when we're alone."
- "I don't like to be alone with [a ministry worker]."
- "[A ministry worker] fooled around with me."

In **"Testimony of a Sex Offender,"** the former convicted pedophile says, "No one plans to become a sex offender." So how does this crime happen? As you'll hear in this DVD segment, it can evolve out of learned behavior—abuse experienced by the predator at an early age, which is then fostered by repeated exposure to pornography. Understanding the mindset of a predator doesn't excuse the crime. But knowing the elements that are commonly present in predators' backgrounds gives us insight into the very real danger of pornography and the insidious impact it can have on individuals and their behavior.

- **View Video #4: "Testimony of a Sex Offender."** *(Similar to "A Victim's Story," Video #4 may be difficult to watch. Although this segment is not graphic in its description of sexual abuse, it may elicit strong emotions if you have experienced abuse or know loved ones who have endured this trauma.)*

Notes:

OPEN FOR DISCUSSION:

- What thoughts and emotions surfaced when you listened to the offender's story?

- Although we never saw the former perpetrator's full image, if you passed him on the street, you would probably never guess that he had committed this crime. Knowing this, what can a ministry do to avoid inadvertently recruiting dangerous workers?

- How equipped do you feel to adequately perform a thorough screening process?

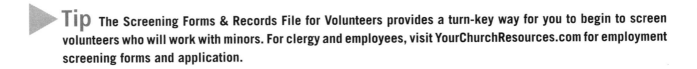

> **Tip** The Screening Forms & Records File for Volunteers provides a turn-key way for you to begin to screen volunteers who will work with minors. For clergy and employees, visit YourChurchResources.com for employment screening forms and application.

o   o   o

Going Deeper o o o o o o

Ward off the opportunists; eliminate the opportunities!

You can learn more about the behavioral profile of a sex offender and find more tools for dealing with sex offenders who are part of your congregation at **ReducingTheRisk.com**. As a ministry leader, your job is not to guess whether a person is a molester or not. Your focus should be on properly screening all candidates, because you cannot tell who is or is not a sex offender.

In addition, solid supervision practices will provide your second layer of defense to deter predators from working in your ministry. Put another way, your job is to ward off the opportunists and eliminate the opportunities!

o   o   o

RELIGIOUS CONVERSION

Should religious conversion make a difference in working with children or youth for individuals who have been guilty of child molestation in the past? Occasionally, such persons freely admit to a prior incident, but now insist that as a result of their conversion experience, they no longer present any risk to children. These individuals should not be allowed to serve in any position with children or youth. The issue is not the person's conversion or salvation, but the safety of the children and the responsibility of ministry leaders. Establishing safe practices for workers is consistent with biblical teaching. The faith community's most important duty is to safeguard children.

Furthermore, from a legal standpoint, a ministry that permits such an individual to work with children or youth—solely on the basis of the professed religious conversion—will have a virtually indefensible position should another incident of molestation occur. These cases can lead to punitive damages for the ministry and personal liability for its leaders.

Fill in the blanks:

Child sexual abuse is not _____.

Child sexual abuse not only affects faith communities _____.

It also destroys _____ and people's _____ in the Church.

Offenders look for _____ environments, and churches are child-nurturing.

Predators _____ children as well as the adult community.

The two-adult rule is for the safety of children and for the protection of _____

against _____.

o   o   o

In Video #5, noted church attorney Richard Hammar makes his case for why screening is critical in safeguarding children from predators. He provides a five-step plan as the basis for your child protection program. Get your pen and workbook ready—you'll want to take notes!

- **View Video #5: "Screening & Selection: Your First Line of Defense (with Richard Hammar)."**

Notes:

- **View Video #6: "Screening & Selection: The Candidate (a short film)."**
Notes:

OPEN FOR DISCUSSION:

- How would you describe the ideal candidate for working with children or youth in your ministry? What characteristics would you want? What would you definitely try to avoid?

- Your role as a leader is not to identify molesters, but rather to eliminate the opportunity for molesters to gain access to kids. How well do your current screening and supervision practices deter sex offenders from trying to serve in your ministries?

- What are Richard Hammar's five steps for a successful child protection program? Which of these five steps are you already doing?

- Would a jury be convinced that your ministry is using reasonable care in the way you select children and youth workers if they scrutinized your screening practices?

Just as a hurdle is an obstacle to a runner, slowing them down, ministries create procedures that present a barrier to potential molesters. The more safeguards that are in place, the lower the risk of possible abuse in your faith community. Here's how ministries reduce opportunities for potential molesters:

1. Application Form

Requiring a written application for volunteers serves the same role as it does for paid employees. The goal is to document the selection process, and to be able to demonstrate that the ministry meets the test of reasonable care. Remember, the focus is not upon the employment status of the worker, but on the worker's responsibilities. A ministry can be just as liable for the negligent selection of a volunteer as it can be for a paid employee. Use the Screening Forms & Records File for Volunteers, and visit **YourChurchResources.com** for employment applications and screening forms for paid staff and clergy.

2. Reference check forms

Ministries should conduct reference checks of all individuals, former employers, and organizations listed for individuals who will work with minors. It is critical that the applicant sign a liability release before the reference checks are done. This provides authorization to conduct reference checks, and releases your references to respond to the request for information. The release should permit you to interview anyone you believe can provide helpful information.

What should you do if a listed reference or former employer refuses to respond? Some organizations refuse to hire a prospective employee in this situation because the failure to respond raises a red flag that requires further exploration. A simple explanation may exist, but in some cases, the reference may not want to share information for fear of being sued.

In certain situations, the concept of "qualified privilege" may also become relevant. Many states recognize a "qualified privilege" on the part of employers to share information about former employees with other employers. This ordinarily means that such statements cannot be the basis for defamation unless they are made with "malice." In this context, malice means either that the former employer knew that the statements made were false, or that statements were made with a reckless disregard as to their truth or falsity. In other words, so long as the reference has a reasonable basis for the statements made about a former worker, the remarks will be protected in many states by a qualified privilege. A local attorney can advise whether or not your state recognizes a qualified privilege under such circumstances.

Important: If you are listed as a reference, and have negative information that you feel compelled to share, make sure that the applicant has signed a liability release. Also, determine whether a qualified privilege exists.

3. Personal interview

A personal interview is an excellent way to gauge a candidate's character and explore their qualifications directly. Information obtained in the reference checks may provide assistance in formulating the interview questions. In addition, other organizations—such as state agencies responsible for investigating reports of child abuse, the school district, Big Brothers, Big Sisters, the Boy Scouts, Girl Scouts, Boys Clubs, Girls Clubs, and the local YMCA or YWCA—may also have materials that can be used to assist staff members who will conduct interviews. Employees of these agencies may be able to provide helpful assistance regarding their own screening process and interview questions.

4. Additional background checks

No court, in any reported decision, has found a church liable on the basis of negligent selection for the molestation of a child on the ground that the church failed to conduct a criminal records check on the molester before using him to work with children. That said, churches that conduct criminal records checks on volunteers who work with minors will be in a better position to defend against an allegation of negligent selection than those who do not conduct such checks. It is worth noting that a growing number of youth-serving organizations are performing criminal records checks on volunteers, and this suggests that the court one day may conclude that "reasonable care" in the selection of children's/youth volunteers necessitates criminal records checks.

Today, such checks can be conducted online. For more information visit **ReducingTheRisk.com**. While a quick check on **nsopr.gov** (National Sex Offender Public Registry) may only take a couple of minutes to receive results, other background searches take longer. There are a variety of criminal records checks available to ministry leaders for screening employees and volunteer workers. These include county, state, and national checks. On their own, no one search provides a complete picture of a person's past. Plus, if you don't know the rules governing which reports you are allowed to use to make a hiring decision, as outlined in the Fair Credit Reporting Act, you can easily misinterpret and misuse the information. We recommend using a reputable background check service provider who can access a full search and interpret the data for you.

The topic of background checks continues to be an area of confusion for many ministries. **ReducingTheRisk.com** provides information to clarify this complex topic and to help you find a reputable background check service provider.

Going Deeper ○ ○ ○ ○ ○ ○
Megan's Laws

The Supreme Court's decision to uphold the constitutionality of state "Megan's Laws" gives youth-serving organizations the ability to perform checks of national and state sex offense registries, such as **nsopr.gov**, without the knowledge or consent of the individual they are checking. As a result, an increasing number of ministries are checking their state sex offender registry for anyone who will have access to minors.

But ministry leaders should be aware of four limitations associated with these checks:

1. Sex offender registries only include convictions for specified sex crimes. Other crimes (kidnapping, murder, assault, etc.) are also relevant in making a decision regarding the suitability of a person to have access to minors.

2. Sex offender registries only contain criminal convictions after a specified date (which in many states is fairly recent).

3. Sex offender registries only include criminal records in one state.

4. Sex offender registries are not easily accessible by the public in some states. For example, in some

states the sex offender registry is maintained by law enforcement agencies, and the public can review the registry only by contacting such an agency.

As a result, ministry leaders should not view a sex offender registry check as the only screening procedure that is necessary. At best, it is one component in an overall screening strategy that includes an application, interview, reference checks, and possibly other criminal records checks.

> **Tip** If you do a sex offender registry search, be sure to retain a copy of the results, even if a person's name is not listed on the registry. This will document that you performed a search, which will be relevant evidence in the event that your ministry is later sued on the basis of negligent selection for the molestation of a child by that person.

What do you do if you discover that your state sex offender registry contains the name of an applicant for youth ministry? First, you need to be absolutely sure that the registry identified the same person as the one you were investigating. In some cases, the registry will contain other identifying information (address, phone number, etc.) that will confirm a person's identity. If not, then call the telephone number listed on the registry website and ask for additional information.

You can quickly find links to the Megan's Law sex offender registries of all 50 states at **klaaskids.org**. Just click on your state and you will be directed to information that is specific to your state, including the name and telephone number of a contact person you can call with any questions; a summary of the kinds of sex offenders who are required to register; and a link to search the registry via the internet (if available).

o   o   o

- **View Video #7: "Legal Requirements: The Church's Responsibility to Protect Kids."**

Notes:

> **Tip** In this DVD segment, Richard Hammar acknowledges that institutions, such as our public school system, interpret the two-adult rule to mean that as long as there is more than one child present, it is acceptable to have only one adult supervising. However, no adult should ever be alone with one child. Some insurance companies and major youth-serving ministries strongly prefer having at least two non-related adults present in all situations. When you establish your ministry's interpretation of the two-adult rule, be sure to enforce it consistently. As Richard Hammar points out, the worst position for a ministry to be in is to have a policy and fail to enforce it consistently.

OPEN FOR DISCUSSION:

- What is your ministry's policy on adult-child supervision?
- Child protection policies should be designed first and foremost with children's safety in mind, not for the convenience of the adults in ministry. Is this true of the policies in your children's ministry?

Fill in the blanks:

The _____ will no longer accept the church's excuse to do _____

to protect children.

NSOPR.gov lists known _____. This is one fast, free, online tool, but it is only one of

many components that should go into a thorough _____ check.

- **View Video #8: "Supervising Scenarios: What Would You Do?"** In this fast-paced motion graphics segment, leaders will have a chance to view several challenging ministry moments. Shout out solutions. But you'll need to think fast—you only get about 30 seconds (usually the amount of time you'll have in real life) to solve each dilemma.

Toddlers:

Preschoolers:

Middle Schoolers:

High Schoolers:

Notes:

OPEN FOR DISCUSSION:

- Which scenario did you find the most difficult to solve?

- What real-world challenges might make it tough for you or your ministry workers to comply with our supervision polices?

- What are the high-risk areas and activities of our ministry?

> **Tip** A youth worker is anyone under age 18 who is volunteering in the children's or youth ministry. Because of their age, they do not qualify as an adult in the two-adult rule.

Going Deeper ○ ○ ○ ○ ○ ○
How Risky Is a Situation?

Not all activities bear the same level of risk. As a result, the level of supervision should correspond to the level of risk. General supervision is appropriate for low-risk activities. But as the risk increases, supervision should increase as well.

But what is it that makes some activities higher risk than others? For example, in general we can say that a "lock-in" represents a higher level of risk than a Sunday school class. But what is it that makes the lock-in a higher risk activity? The answer lies in three factors: Isolation, accountability, and power.

The safest environment is one with low isolation, high accountability, and a balance of power. Molesters, on the other hand, look for programs with increased isolation, lower accountability, and opportunities to maintain power over their victims.

By analyzing the degree of isolation, accountability, and power in any given situation, you can quickly adjust your supervision level to lower the level of risk for something going wrong.

Risk Factor 1: Isolation

Risk increases as isolation increases.

Most, but not all, sexual abuse occurs in isolated settings. Four factors affect isolation: (1) the number of people present, (2) the time of the activity, (3) the location of the activity, and (4) the physical arrangements. Let's practice applying these principles:

> **Example:** *Two adults and one youth worker are serving in the nursery during the 9 a.m. service. Two babies are asleep in cribs, and four infants are laying on baby play mats while the workers sit next to them on the floor. One baby wakes up and needs a diaper change, so one adult volunteer brings her to the changing table in the far corner of the room. The second baby wakes up and begins to cry, so the other adult picks up this baby to comfort her and walks out of the room to avoid setting off a chain reaction of crying babies. That leaves the 13-year-old youth worker watching four babies.*

In this example, isolation is low initially. The nursery is well-supervised—until the two adults get called away to tend to the babies. At this point, the nursery now poses a higher level of risk for the infants and the workers. The youth worker is too distracted trying to monitor the four babies she is now in charge of that she fails to notice the woman changing the baby's diaper in the corner. Diapering—or any other bathroom-related tasks—should never be done in isolation. It leaves the child dangerously vulnerable, plus it puts the ministry worker in a position where no one can vouch for her actions. Also, with a 13-year-old youth worker and an adult worker, there is a disparity of age between volunteers. It is highly unlikely that the student worker will speak up if something seems out of place with her superior, let alone know to hold an adult accountable for her actions. And finally, while the likelihood of a woman being a sex offender is low (studies estimate that approximately 94 percent of all perpetrators of sexual abuse are male), it does occur. Remember, you can't tell by looking at someone whether he or she is a sex offender.

A safer solution for this nursery example would have been for the woman with the crying baby to call for back-up and request that another adult step in until she can calm the crying baby. Or she could have remained just outside the door where she could monitor the youth worker and the woman changing the diaper until she was finished. The goal should always be to create settings where isolation is eliminated and accountability exists.

> **Example:** *Teachers invite their Sunday morning class to return to the church on Sunday afternoon at 3 p.m. for a party. No other activities are present on church property at that time.*

In this example, the children meet in the same location in the afternoon as they did in the morning. The change in time, however, alters the number of people present in the building. As a result, the risk environment has changed. Isolation has increased, so risk has also increased. This means the supervision should also increase and become more accountable—having at least two non-related adults present, for example, as well as having approval to sponsor the activity.

Let's look at another variation of this example. What if the party occurs at a local restaurant rather than at the church? The typical restaurant does not represent isolated space. However, other risks are present, including transportation to and from the restaurant. In addition, other safety factors require the need for two or more adults for any activity that is held off of church property. If one adult becomes unavailable for any reason, a second adult will be needed.

 Tip Any activity that is deemed "higher risk" should have two or more non-related adults as supervisors.

Risk Factor 2: Accountability

Risk increases as accountability decreases.

The sexual abuse of children always occurs in settings without proper accountability. Notice the relationship between risk and accountability in each of the following examples.

—*Fred, a college student and a volunteer worker with the church's high school youth group, announces he is available for transportation if any of the members need a ride to group activities. Anne, a 17–year-old high school senior, asks Fred for a ride.*

—*Stan, the new youth pastor, wants to meet with members of the youth group to get to know them better. He decides to pick up students after school and take them out to get some ice cream. However, church policy requires that he must obtain permission in advance for such meetings. The pastor decides that another youth supervisor must be present.*

—*Randy, an adult member of First Church, volunteers to pick up a 10-year-old boy on his way to church each week. The boy lives with his mother, who is delighted to have a "father figure" express an interest in her son.*

In the three examples above, only the middle one demonstrates the use of accountability. Accountability involves justifying one's actions. Since sexual molestation cannot be justified, the perpetrators of abuse avoid settings in which they must give an account of their behavior. That's why they seek isolated settings, act in secrecy, and attempt to maintain power and control over their victims. Also, some workers, although they have had no prior intent on engaging in misconduct, may nevertheless cross a boundary under certain circumstances. Supervision policies that require accountability help reduce opportunities for exploiting kids. Three factors affect the accountability of supervisors in ministry programs involving children: (1) the personal character and integrity of the adult worker, (2) the number of people present for the activity, and (3) the degree of openness and approval associated with the activity.

Let's take a closer look at each factor.

1. *Personal character and integrity.* Clearly, a person's character and integrity affect risk, and that is why screening workers is a vital part of a prevention program. Parents assume that their children will be safe when they leave them in the care of another adult. Embedded in that assumption is that the adult is trustworthy and has the best interests of the children at heart. Unfortunately, as the events of recent years have demonstrated, that assumption is not always true. As a result,

reasonable care means that individuals who work with children need to be screened. The goal is to gain assurance that individuals have been accountable in the past and are likely to be accountable in the future.

2. *The number of people present.* As a general rule: the more adults, the better. Accountability increases when two or more non-related adults are present for activities that involve children and youth. Having multiple adults present decreases the risk of isolation and helps to maintain a better balance of power and control.

   It is also a good idea to use a "building monitor" to inspect vacant rooms, buildings that are set apart, and private areas such as restrooms. People are less likely to engage in inappropriate conduct if they think someone is watching.

3. *Degree of openness and approval.* Openness is also important for accountability to occur. Ministry leaders should be fully aware of all activities in advance, and approve the content, activities, and leadership of each program. Individuals acting in secrecy raise immediate red flags. All activities sponsored by the ministry or that take place on ministry property require advance approval. Other factors such as lighting, windows, open doors, and the use of video surveillance equipment can enhance the level of openness and reduce secrecy of activities that occur on ministry property.

Let's now use the risk factors of isolation and accountability to analyze the following example.

> **Example:** *A fourth grade Sunday school class has two non-related adult teachers. The class meets at the home of one of the teachers on a Friday night from 7-9 p.m. to play volleyball. Both teachers are present, and parents are also invited to attend. The Christian Education Director has approved the activity. Both teachers went through a screening program before they began working with children.*

The first point to notice is the event is being held off of church property, which makes it higher risk. This triggers the need for two or more non-related adults, such as the two teachers. Parents are also invited to attend, which further lowers isolation and increases accountability. Risk decreases even further since both teachers have gone through a screening process.

In this example, the risk of abuse is relatively low, yet other factors can contribute to a dynamic risk environment, which can change at any moment. Imagine, for example, that one child gets another child alone in a bedroom while everyone else plays outside. Abuse could occur in that isolated setting. To avoid such a scenario, boundaries should be established concerning the use of the house. Furthermore, those responsible for supervision should be aware of such concerns and take appropriate actions to monitor the space and maintain an open environment that facilitates low risk.

Next, let's create a few variations in this example to show how easily the risk environment can be altered. First, suppose parents are not invited. Second, only one teacher is present. Third, no one on the church staff knows about the event. Fourth, no screening occurred, and the teacher has a criminal record that no one knows about. Fifth, the time is extended to 11 p.m. Sixth, only boys are invited, and the event includes a sleepover. Each of these factors increases the level of risk as isolation is increased and accountability is decreased.

Let's now look at the third risk factor—the level of power that exists.

Risk Factor 3: Power

Risk increases when there is an imbalance of power, authority, influence, and control between a potential abuser and a potential victim.

One reason that children are so vulnerable to sexual predators is the imbalance of power related to age, size, strength, and also control and authority. Most child victims of sexual abuse know and trust their abuser. They may also fear the person. Once abuse occurs, perpetrators will use their power, authority, and influence to promote silence.

Control can be exerted in many ways, both physically and psychologically. Some abusers use "grooming" techniques to gain the trust and control of a child. They may offer cash, gifts, trips, fun experiences, and shower the child with attention and favors. They may also use blackmail, threats, physical force, and intimidation. In addition, predatory abusers often select their victims carefully to increase their likelihood of success. Children who are targets for abuse are no match for such predators.

What makes the problem unusually difficult in ministry settings is that the abuser is often a respected member of the faith community. Often, these individuals will also use their spiritual authority as a means of power and control. Ministry leaders and parents are sometimes slow to see the signs of abuse because they, too, may trust and respect the abuser.

Abuse is less likely to occur when a balance of power exists. A growing number of ministry-related abuse cases involve another minor as the perpetrator of the abuse. In part, these cases occur because of an imbalance of power, which is typically age-related. It is less common, for example, for a 9-year-old to molest another 9-year-old than for a 15-year-old to molest a 7-year-old.

MINISTRY ACTIVITIES

By their very nature, some activities represent a higher level of risk for sexual molestation than do others. These activities often increase isolation and lower accountability. Ministry leaders should pay careful attention to and increase supervision for the following events:

- Any activity that occurs in a home

- Any overnight activity, including lock-ins, camping trips, or staying in a hotel

- Any activity that involves changing clothes or becoming undressed, such as in locker rooms or dressing rooms

- Any activity that involves groups of children with age differences of four years or more

- Any activity that occurs in a natural, isolated environment, such as a building that is set off by itself, or a park that has secluded areas

Consider the following two scenarios in light of the three risk factors of isolation, accountability, and power.

Scenario 1: *The youth pastor picks up one or more youth members in his car. Sometimes the meetings are directly after school, other times they are at night or on a weekend. Many of the meetings are at the youth pastor's apartment. Sometimes he takes the students to a movie or athletic event. He gives the girls candy and* *the boys t-shirts. Church leaders think the discipleship program is a good idea, but no one knows any details about the program. Some of the parents have never met the youth pastor since they do not attend church. Some of the single parents think he is great because he serves as a wonderful role model for their children. He even offers to let them stay all night at his apartment if the single parent has to go out of town.*

Scenario 2: *The meetings occur at the church during regular office hours. Other staff members are present in the building. No meeting is one-on-one. Instead, they occur in the church library with the youth pastor and youth members seated at a table. The library door is open and the church receptionist is directly across the hall. The senior pastor has approved the discipleship effort. The schedule of meetings is made through the church receptionist on a monthly basis, and a copy of the schedule is given to the participants, their parents, and the pastor. The youth pastor was screened before being hired, including a criminal records check. The church has a policy that the youth pastor may not individually socialize with any member of the youth group, invite individuals to his home, or give any individual member a gift without the knowledge of the pastor. All parents are asked to sign a permission form before their child can participate in the discipleship program.*

The programs in Scenarios 1 and 2 could both potentially result in very effective and rewarding discipleship efforts. The difference is that Scenario 1 is a high-risk environment that could just as easily result in child sexual abuse with catastrophic results for the child, the child's family, the youth pastor, the church leadership, and the entire congregation.

Let's look at another example:

Example: *First Church sponsors a scouting program for boys. This weekend the boys will be at a wilderness campground using pup tents with two persons to a tent.*

Consider the following two scenarios for this example:

Scenario 1: *The Sunday before the campout, the scoutmaster announces to the congregation that they may have to cancel the trip because they still need two men to serve as supervisors. He asks if anyone is interested in helping, and if so, they should contact him following the service. Randy, a single man who began attending the church several weeks ago, volunteers to help. He's excited about being a part of the program and was an Eagle Scout himself. The scoutmaster also recruits one of his colleagues from work who enjoys the outdoors and has a son of his own who will go on the trip. It turns out the church has exactly enough tents to accommodate two people per tent. Randy shares a tent with a 13-year-old boy. When they arrive at the camp, the boys are given a few hours to go exploring.*

Scenario 2: *Nine boys and three adult supervisors attend the campout. Each of the supervisors has completed a screening form and has been a member of the church for more than six months. Parents of the boys have all attended an orientation meeting. All the boys, parents, and supervisors are asked to sign an honor code, which explains and stipulates a code of behavior that is to be followed while on the trip. When they arrive at the campground, clear instructions are provided concerning where they can go, and under what circumstances. Each supervisor has clearly defined responsibilities. Two boys of the same approximate age are assigned to each tent. One three-person tent is used to accommodate three boys. The adult supervisors also sleep together in a larger tent. A curfew is in effect once lights are out.*

Based on the three risk factors, we recognize that both scenarios represent a high-risk program, with a dynamic, changing risk environment. Isolation is high; the program occurs overnight; the activities represent higher levels of risk; the potential for secrecy exists; and power differences are present. A need exists to lower isolation, increase accountability, balance power, and maintain specific supervision to observe and control activities.

Nothing in Scenario 1 indicates awareness of the three risk factors. The scoutmaster begins with a high-risk activity and makes it worse through his own actions. Rather than lowering isolation, he increases it as the boys go exploring. Rather than increasing accountability, he decreases it by recruiting supervisors that have not been properly screened. Rather than balancing power, he creates an imbalance by having an adult sleep alone with a child in the same tent. Nothing indicates an understanding of the risk of child sexual abuse, or the steps that can be taken to lower that risk.

Scenario 2 reflects fundamental principles of risk management. Isolation is reduced through the use of boundary conditions, including a curfew. The use of an honor code, an orientation meeting, and screening increases accountability. Sleeping arrangements are planned to maintain a balance of power. Even though these measures have been taken, abuse could still occur. But the church has taken significant steps to reduce that risk. If an allegation of negligent supervision occurred, the church would be able to defend itself using a coherent strategy of care grounded in identifiable principles of risk management.

▶ *Action Item:*

It is important that all ministry leaders be able to assess levels of risk and understand how to lower risk through adjustments in the nature of the supervision that is provided. To practice this, select one or more of your ministry activities. Assess the risk level using the factors of isolation, accountability, and power. Identify steps that can be taken to lower risk.

Fill in the blanks:

The _____ rule is the first principle of supervision.

Three factors that determine the level of risk are _____, _____, and

_____.

When sitting with toddlers, always avoid placing a child in a way that covers your _____.

Disparity in power increases as the gap in _____, _____, and level of authority widens.

o   o   o

Ministry leaders need to know how to report a suspected case of child sexual abuse in the church, and how to respond to any allegation that is brought forth. The next video, **"Responding to an Allegation,"** walks you through the best way to handle these situations.

- **View Video #9: "Responding to an Allegation."**

Notes:

OPEN FOR DISCUSSION:

- Now that you've seen this DVD segment, how would you respond to an allegation?

- How would you have responded to the parents' first phone call about the youth pastor instant messaging their daughter?

- What steps of responding to an allegation would be the hardest for you to enforce, and why?

Going Deeper ∘ ∘ ∘ ∘ ∘ ∘
Handling an Incident

Not only must a ministry do all it can to prevent abuse; it must also be prepared to respond if a reported case of abuse should occur. Every worker should be equipped to know when and how to report any suspicious activities. Here are some guidelines that will be helpful in understanding how to handle an incident of sexual abuse in your ministry.

DISCUSS SUSPICIOUS BEHAVIOR IMMEDIATELY

Any inappropriate conduct or relationships between an adult worker and a member of the youth group or a child should be confronted immediately and investigated. Issue a prompt warning, or if necessary, terminate the adult worker's services immediately if the violation is of sufficient gravity. Ministry staff should note when a member of the youth group appears aloof or withdrawn, or exhibits a marked personality change. This may indicate a problem that deserves attention.

Some types of conduct only require an initial comment or warning:

Example: *The church youth group is having a picnic at a local lake. Following a volleyball game, one of the male chaperones begins to massage the shoulders of one of the female youth members. They are seated at a picnic table surrounded by other students. A second adult chaperone discretely pulls the first one aside and comments, "You probably weren't aware, but giving massages falls outside of proper volunteer conduct."*

Other types of conduct require immediate reporting:

Example: *The same facts as the preceding example, but the volunteer worker walks the student to an isolated location and massages her shoulders while laying down on the ground next to her. A second volunteer sees what is happening and immediately reports it to the adult in charge.*

Example: *A male youth volunteer is seen kissing a female member of the youth group. The action is immediately reported to the pastor.*

DISCUSS POTENTIAL CRIMINAL SANCTIONS WITH YOUTH WORKERS

Adults who work with children and adolescent youth should understand that sexual relationships with minors could lead to a felony conviction and imprisonment in a state penitentiary. The law views such misconduct very seriously, as it should. Children's/Youth workers also need to understand that the insurance policy will not provide them with a legal defense in the case of a sexual misconduct charge, or pay any portion of a jury verdict assessed against them on account of such conduct.

MONITOR FACILITIES AND CREATE OPEN ENVIRONMENTS

Appoint a person to monitor the facilities during services and activities. Sunday school superintendents or other ministry leaders also should make random visits to all classrooms and frequently visit or inspect areas of buildings that are isolated. If feasible, consider installing windows on the doors to all classrooms or other areas used by minors. The windows should be made out of shatterproof glass. Alternatively, the doors to such classrooms should be left open during use so that persons passing by can observe what is happening inside. Some ministries also use video systems to monitor facilities.

ESTABLISH SAFEGUARDS FOR ARRIVAL AND DISMISSAL

It's necessary to establish guidelines so that children are not left unsupervised prior to or following ministry activities.

USE A NURSERY IDENTIFICATION PROCEDURE

Procedures should exist for the nursery that clearly identifies the child and the child's parent or guardian. Children should only be released to a properly identified and preauthorized adult.

DISCUSS APPROPRIATE AND INAPPROPRIATE TOUCHING

Touching should always be age-appropriate and based on the need of the child, not the need of the adult.

Clearly, touching is an important way of showing comfort and affection to small children. But it should only be done in response to the child's need.

Example: *Sarah, a 2-year old, falls down and scratches her knee and begins to cry. Jean, one of the nursery attendants, places Sarah next to her so they can sit close to each other. This is an example of appropriate touching.*

Example: *Paul, an adult youth supervisor, wraps his arms around the waist of a 14-year-old girl at a church youth activity. This is an example of inappropriate touching.*

MUTUAL ACCOUNTABILITY — A MINISTRY OBLIGATION

Questionable or inappropriate behavior often precedes acts of child molestation. You are encouraged to identify and alert your leader when questionable behavior is displayed, and to report such behavior to the proper individuals. Holding co-workers accountable, done with care and sensitivity, can help to avoid actual instances of abuse or molestation.

PERSONAL RESPONSIBILITY — A MORAL OBLIGATION

Workers sometimes fail to report a suspected incident of child sexual abuse for a variety of reasons. Some may want to avoid embarrassing situations, or a fear of possible personal and legal recrimination may exist. Nevertheless, discrete and confidential reporting of suspected abuse is critical to abuse prevention. Reporting reflects caring and is not an act of disloyalty.

MINISTRY REPORTING PROCEDURE

Your ministry should develop clear instructions concerning when a report should occur and how it should be made. Here are some additional factors to consider in deciding whether or not to report a suspected incident of abuse to the state:

1. **Are you a mandatory or permissive reporter under state law?** Mandatory reporters (as defined by state law) face criminal penalties for not reporting. Permissive reporters are permitted to report but they are not legally required to do so. However, it is possible that permissive reporters who do not report reasonable suspicions of abuse will be sued later by victims who allege that their suffering was perpetuated by the failure to report. Therefore, do not automatically dismiss a duty to report on the ground that you are a permissive reporter under state law.

2. **What is the definition of child abuse in my state?** Some states define abuse very narrowly to include only abuse inflicted by a parent or caretaker. Be sure you know how your state defines child abuse.

3. **Do I have reasonable cause to believe that abuse has occurred?** Remember, most state laws require mandatory reporters to report not only actual abuse, but also reasonable suspicions of abuse. Our recommendation—interpret "reasonable cause" very broadly. Also, note that child abusers, when confronted with their misconduct, often deny it. Any allegation must be treated seriously.

4. **Be especially aggressive when dealing with pedophilic behavior** (that is, sexual molestation of a pre-adolescent child). Some studies suggest that a pedophile may have hundreds of victims over the course of a lifetime. You have a duty to protect other innocent victims. Resolve doubts in favor of reporting.

5. **Be especially aggressive when dealing with suspected abuse on the part of a person with a history of previous abusive behavior.** Resolve doubts in favor of reporting.

6. **Does the clergy-penitent privilege apply?** In a few states, clergy who learn of child abuse during a confidential counseling session are not required to report the information to the state.

7. **Consider discussing the case anonymously with a representative of the state agency that receives reports of abuse.** These representatives often are more than willing to discuss particular cases and evaluate whether or not a report should be filed. Of course, if you are advised that a report need not be filed, be sure to obtain the representative's name and make a record of the call.

8. **Consider filing an anonymous report from the office of some independent third party** (such as a local attorney or the pastor of another church). The other person can later verify that you in fact made the report.

9. **If you have any doubts concerning your duty to report a particular incident to the state, an attorney should be consulted.** It is also desirable to inform your ministry's insurance agent.

Fill in the blanks:

Any inappropriate _____ or relationships between an adult worker and a member of the

youth group or a child should be _____ immediately and investigated.

Reporting an incident of inappropriate behavior by another leader toward a child reflects _____

and is not an act of _____.

Ministry workers should be aware of _____ laws that govern the reporting of child abuse.

■ **View Video #10: "Take the Next Steps."**

This training is merely a first step toward raising awareness for the importance of protecting kids from sexual abuse, and for practical ways to implement a child protection program.

Notes:

OPEN FOR DISCUSSION:

- What key take-away points did you gain from the Training DVD?

- After seeing the entire Training DVD, where do you stand in your commitment to safeguard children in your ministry from becoming victims of sexual abuse?

- What obstacles or concerns do you still have about being able to implement a more consistent, thorough approach to screening and supervising workers?

- What changes will you need to make in order to follow the full screening process—including application, interview, references, background checks, and the *Reducing the Risk* training program?

After you have completed all of the Reducing the Risk *Training DVD segments and have read the* **Trainee Workbook** *that pertains to your ministry role, you are ready to take your test. Please go to the back of the* **Trainee Workbook** *and tear out this test. When you have finished it, turn it in to your supervisor. You may be asked to repeat this training periodically.*

CHAPTER TWO

For Children's/ Youth Workers:

KEEPING KIDS SAFE

Practical Ways to Protect Children

"See that you do not look down on one of these little ones. For I tell you that their angels in heaven always see the face of my Father in heaven." (Matthew 18:10)

You serve in this ministry because you love kids. Nothing satisfies a committed children's worker more than seeing a child grow in Christ. Real spiritual growth can only take place in a safe environment—a place where kids' questions and their journey to God are honored and protected. This child protection training will teach you about the very real problem of child sexual abuse and its devastating effects in faith communities. Thankfully, there is hope. Because of people like you, children in ministry programs everywhere are better protected. The same love that compelled you to answer the call to serve in this ministry is the love that will inspire you to implement the protection policies you'll learn here.

Training Overview
For Children's/Youth Workers (approximately 2 hours)

WHAT'S THE GOAL OF THIS TRAINING?

- To train children's/youth ministry workers on your child protection principles.
- To inspire ministry workers to keep kids safe at church.

WHO SHOULD ATTEND?

- All workers of programs geared toward children and youth—whether full-time or occasional—should attend this session.

WHAT WILL I NEED TO PARTICIPATE IN THIS TRAINING?

- *Reducing the Risk* Training DVD, or online access to **ReducingTheRisk.com** for individual training
- *Reducing the Risk* Trainee Workbook and pen

Let's Get Started

Today, you'll learn about the problem of child sexual abuse in ministries and how to keep kids safe from this tragedy. Keeping kids safe is the first priority of children's/youth ministries. If children aren't safe, whether physically, emotionally, mentally, or spiritually—you can't effectively minister to them.

■ **View Video #1: "Child Protection as the Foundation of Your Ministry."**

Notes:

■ **View Video #2: "A Victim's Story."**

Notes:

OPEN FOR DISCUSSION:

■ Why did you choose to serve in children's or youth ministry?

■ Based on the first two DVD segments, what initial impressions do you have about our efforts to provide a safe environment for children?

■ What should children and their parents reasonably expect from us as children's/youth workers when they participate in our programs?

■ How did the **"Victim's Story"** make you feel? What parts of that DVD segment especially stood out to you?

Fill in the blanks:

When it comes to _____, many people still don't believe that the

_____ is real.

When a child has a good ministry experience, he is more likely to _____ in his faith and

stay involved with the _____. When a child is a victim of sexual abuse in a

faith community, the _____ are devastating and last the child's _____.

Our ministry is committed to being the safest place on Earth for children to grow in their faith. The first way we practice this principle is by following a consistent, thorough screening process. The second step we take toward safeguarding kids is establishing policies for supervision. Our next DVD segment will highlight several common scenarios you're likely to encounter in ministry, and you'll have a chance as a group to brainstorm solutions in between each scene.

- ■ **View Video #8: "Supervising Scenarios: What Would You Do?"**

Notes:

The Toddler Room: *What would you do?*

Preschoolers: *What would you do?*

Middle Schoolers: *What would you do?*

High Schoolers: *What would you do?*

Now that you've considered each of the scenarios in the video, let's look at our ministry's supervision policies and guidelines, and expectations for behavior by leaders.

Fill in the blanks:

Our ministry's supervision policies include: _____.

I am expected to: _____.

The three factors that determine the level of risk include _____, _____, and

_____.

Let's practice using supervision principles on one more scenario. Analyze the situation using the three risk factors of isolation, accountability, and power.

> **Example:** *You serve as a volunteer worker with the high school ministry. The pastor introduces you to Brett, a son of committed church members, who has come home from college to be a summer ministry intern. Three weeks later, your group has a day-long outing at the lake. Several times you notice that, while Brett plays in the lake with a group of kids, a lot of physical contact with several girls occurs. Later in the day you notice Brett giving a neck massage to a girl during a rest period.*

- Does such behavior warrant any response?

- What should you do after witnessing Brett's behavior?

Going Deeper ○ ○ ○ ○ ○ ○
Reporting Procedures for Children's/Youth Workers

Child sexual abuse thrives when it goes unnoticed or unreported. Often, an abusive situation continues because of someone's failure to report it. As a children's/youth worker you need to know what constitutes an occasion for reporting, the reporting channels you should use, and your obligations to make a report.

REPORTING OBLIGATIONS

An effective reporting procedure enhances the effort to protect children. Ordinarily, child molesters will not remain in a ministry where workers are trained to identify symptoms of child abuse and are encouraged to report suspicious behavior. Child abusers thrive on secrecy and are more likely to commit criminal acts in organizations where they go unnoticed.

STATE COMPLIANCE—A LEGAL OBLIGATION

Every state has a mandatory reporting law that specifies the following:

- What constitutes child abuse.

- Those persons ("mandatory reporters") who are legally responsible for reporting known and reasonably suspected cases of abuse. Most states require a direct report to a state agency.

- The length of time required to make a report. In most states, those providing professional care or services to children have a 48-hour period to make a report. In some states, an oral report is due within 24 hours.

- The nature and content of the report. Many states permit the reporter to remain anonymous. However, if an individual desires to remain anonymous, the report should be made over the phone in the presence of an attorney or other independent witness who can verify later, if necessary, the identity of the reporter. This may become important if the reporter later is charged with negligence for failing to make a report. If no witnesses to the report exist, and the report is done anonymously, providing a defense becomes problematic.

- The social agencies or department to be contacted. In some states, reports can made to law enforcement officers.

- The criminal penalties for failing to report. Failure to report may be punishable by a fine or jail sentence.

- Protection from legal and civil litigation if the report is made in good faith.

▶ **Tip** Be sure to check your state child abuse reporting laws regularly. State legislatures tend to amend these laws often, and children's/youth workers need to be aware of any such changes. Richard Hammar publishes an annual state-by-state listing of child sexual abuse reporting laws. Visit *ReducingTheRisk.com* for more information.

o　o　o

- **View Video #9: "Responding to an Allegation."**

Notes:

- In **"Responding to an Allegation,"** Jasmine recounted the steps she and her church took in order to respond to an allegation of an abuse with a youth worker and a young girl. How would you have responded to these allegations?

- Who would you report an incident to if you suspected a child had been abused by a co-worker in your ministry?

- **View Video #10: "Taking the Next Step."**

Notes:

PERSONAL COMMITMENT

Congratulations! You've just completed one of the most important training opportunities of your ministry. Please take a minute to reflect on your personal commitment to protecting children from being abused in our ministry. The final step in your training is to take the test at the back of this book. Please tear it out and turn in your completed test to your supervisor. You may be asked to repeat child protection training periodically.

PREVENTING CHILD SEXUAL ABUSE TEST:

Please indicate whether the following statements are true or false.

1. Child sexual abuse always involves physical contact with children.
    ☐ **true**   ☐ **false**

2. Most child molesters are male.
    ☐ **true**   ☐ **false**

3. Child molesters are usually strangers to the victim.
    ☐ **true**   ☐ **false**

4. Victims of sexual abuse suffer no long-term effects.
    ☐ **true**   ☐ **false**

5. Most ministries screen workers for potential molesters.
    ☐ **true**   ☐ **false**

6. Ministry leaders cannot be held liable for child sexual abuse.
    ☐ **true**   ☐ **false**

7. A child molester who has experienced a religious conversion no longer presents a threat to children.
    ☐ **true**   ☐ **false**

Choose the correct answers for the following questions.

10.Which of the following are risk factors as they pertain to supervision?
    a) **isolation**
    b) **arrogance**
    c) **small rooms**
    d) **accountability**
    e) **power**

11. When a child has been abused, or an accusation has been made, what are the ministry's next steps?

    a) take it seriously

    b) document the allegation

    c) take it to a state agency

    d) provide support for the victim

    e) all of the above

12. *(For Ministry Leaders only)* What four steps should every ministry take during the screening process?

    a) personal interview

    b) give a written test

    c) reference checks

    d) written application

    e) observe applicant with children

    f) background check

Answer the following questions. (For Ministry Leaders only)

13. What makes a ministry susceptible to sex offenders?

14. Who do sex offenders "groom" as discussed in the Roundtable video segment?

15. What is one thing you've learned about ministry liability concerning child sexual abuse?

Upon completion of this test, tear it out and turn it in to your supervisor.

Allegation Response Checklist

If your ministry is accused of child sexual abuse, use the following checklist to ensure that your response is appropriate and legal.

☐ We have taken all allegations seriously, and have not engaged in denial, minimization, or blame. We have followed up on all allegations.

☐ We collected in writing all relevant information concerning the allegation.

☐ We promptly fulfilled any state reporting obligation concerning the alleged child abuse.

☐ We notified our insurance agent, appropriate judicatory leaders, and our attorney concerning the allegation.

☐ We have placed appropriate restrictions on alleged perpetrators of misconduct until the case is resolved.

☐ We have maintained strict confidentiality concerning all information, and will communicate with congregational members on the basis of their need to know under the restrictions of a qualified privilege.

☐ We are providing support to the victim and the victim's family.

MAKE THE BEST USE OF THIS RESOURCE

BY USING IT WITH ALL MATERIALS FROM THE FULL KIT

"Ministry leadership today requires deliberate, consistent, and steadfast passion for kids' safety. **Reducing the Risk** will help you ignite th[e] passion and take prov[en] steps toward protecti[ng] your church's childre[n] and youth."

DAVID STAAL Promisela[nd] Director, Willow Creek Community Church

REDUCING THE RISK
3rd EDITION

PRICING INFORMATION:

ITEM #L324: **Reducing the Risk** *Training DVD* **$69.95**

ITEM #L323: **Reducing the Risk** *Leader's Guide* **$29.95**

ITEM #L322*: **Reducing the Risk** *Trainee Workbook* **$6.50**

ITEM #L321*: **Reducing the Risk** *Screening Forms & Records File for Volunteers* **$4.50**

SPECIAL COMBO OFFERS:

ITEM #L320S: **Reducing the Risk** *Kit* (includes 1 Training DVD, 1 Leader's Guide, 10 Trainee Workbooks, and 10 Screening Forms & Records Files for Volunteers) *SPECIAL OFFER* **$149.95** *(more than a 25% savings)*

ITEM #L322S: **Reducing the Risk** *Trainee Refill* (includes 10 Trainee Workbooks and 10 Screening Forms & Records Files for Volunteers) **$79.95** *(more than a 25% savings)*

ITEM #L323S: **Reducing the Risk** *Leader's Starter Kit* (includes 1 Training DVD, 1 Leader's Guide, 1 Trainee Workbook, and 1 Screening Forms & Records File for Volunteers) **$89.95** *(more than a 15% savings)*

For discounted packs of 10 visit YourChurchCatalog.com

Pricing is subject to change

Reducing the Risk
3rd Edition

RICHARD [F.] **HAMMAR,** J. D., LL.M. CPA